NARRATIVE

OF

HENRY BIRD,

Who was carried away by the Indians, after the murder of his whole family, in 1811, and held in Captivity:—His sufferings, and rescue from the Savage Monsters, in 1815, while burning at the stake.

PRINTED AT BRIDGEPORT, NOVEMBER 1815.

NARRATIVE

OF

HENRY BIRD,

Who was carried away by the Indians, after the murder of his whole family, in 1811, and held in Captivity:—His sufferings, and rescue from the Savage Monsters, in 1815, while burning at the stake.

PRINTED AT BRIDGEPORT, NOVEMBER 1815.

NARRATIVE of HENRY BIRD

When white and Indian culture clashed on the American frontier there were many incidents where men, women and children were captured by Indians. Many were ransomed, some were voluntarily returned, more than a few escaped, all had adventures to tell about. The story of Henry Bird is unusual but is believed to be true. Crudely printed 158 years ago the original is now rare.

NARRATIVE

of

Henry Bird

Who was carried away by the Indians,
after the murder of his whole
family in 1811.

YE GALLEON PRESS

Fairfield, Washington

1973

ISBN 0·87770·115·6

NARRATIVE

of

HENRY BIRD

Henry Bird removed in 1797 from Fredrick county, Virginia, where he was born in 1767, to the head waters of Sandusky, in the state of Ohio. He was accompanied by two of his neighbours, John Peters and Thomas Philips, in partnership with whom he had purchased a little tract of six hundred and sixty acres of land. At that time there were no inhabitants within eight or nine miles of the spot they had chosen. The first thing they did was to build a log hut, with the assistance of their neighbours, who each brought a bushel of wheat to support the new comers until they could raise their own grain. Such is the custom in all these little frontier settlements, where necessity has revived many good old patriarchal customs, and established a neighbourly connexion among the first settlers that is not seen in other communities.

Narrative of Henry Bird

Here Bird lived till the year 1811, during which time he became the father of five children, and saw the country change from a wilderness inhabited by panthers, bears, buffaloes, wolves and wild turkeys, to cultivated farms, belonging to sturdy, independent yeomanry.

The first year he came, though no hunter, he killed two panthers, and had an irruption made into his pig-sty, which adjoined one end of his hut, by a bear, which carried off one of his pigs. For a long time he was disturbed at night by the howling of wolves close under his windows; but as the country became cleared and more thickly settled, they gradually receded into the woods, and seldom came near the house. The Indians were all about them, and a friendly intercourse had long subsisted between Bird, and a warrior of the Shawanese tribe, called the Big Captain, who often came and slept at his house.

But after the battle of Tippecanoe, they all disappeared; and as this was a signal that they meditated revenge, the inhabitants gathered together, two or three families in a hut, that they might be the better able to resist any sudden attack. Bird's friends, Peters and Philips, came to his house with their families, because it was larger than theirs, having, as he says, "two fire-places with a partition between." The whole number thus collected amounted to nineteen, three men, three women, and thirteen children some of them quite grown up.

On the 17th of October, 1811, "just after day-light was gone," to use his own expressions, while Bird was lying down on the bed, his wife roasted a piece of buffaloe, and Peters and Philips, with three of the daughters were sitting round the fire, eight guns were discharged through the window, which killed the whole party at the fire, and wounded Bird in the hip with two balls. He sprung out of bed, but dropped on the floor, and at the same instant the Indians , eighteen in number, burst open the door with a horrible yell. Bird endeavoured to climb up so as to reach one of four loaded muskets, which hung against the wall, but was followed by an Indian who struck him in the shoulder with his tomahawk. This blow brought him down, and the Indian cut and hacked away at his left side which was upppermost, until he thought him quite dead. Then, having killed the whole nineteen, and being fearful that the firing might have roused the neighborhood, they seized the four rifles, the Big Captain gave the retreating war whoop, and they all retired to their canoes, which had been left at the head of a creek communicating with the waters of the Great Sandusky.

Here they lay until morning, when finding all quiet, they returned to the house and fell to stripping the dead bodies, amounting to eighteen. When they had done this, they piled them up in the middle of the room. The Indians attempted to strip off Bird's hunting shirt of tow-linen, and were going to scalp him and throw him on the pile with the rest, when the Big Captain came. Bird spoke to him by name, begged to be tomahawked, and told the Captain "he never used him so when he came to see him." The Big Captain then without making any reply, began to examine his wounds, which, when he had done, he exclaimed with wonder, "that the Great Spirit would not let him die. I will carry you home and cure you," said he.

He ordered two Indians to put Bird in a blanket and carry him down to his canoe, whither he followed him; and while the rest of the party were bringing down the plunder, dressed his wounds; for the Indians always carry with them materials for dressing wounds when they go to war. By this time they had loaded their canoes, and when the last party left the house, they set it on fire in order to burn the dead bodies, among which were Bird's wife and five children. This done they went down the Sandusky into lake Erie, which they crossed and coasted down to the lower end, till they came to a creek the Indians called *To koh;* up which they proceeded about fourteen miles to the old Shawanese town. This was a distance near four hundred miles; during all this time the Big Captain dressed Bird's wounds with considerable skill, but handled him so roughly as to put him to very great pain. Bird thinks he remembers every thing that passed in this long transportation; and when I asked him about his state of mind, said "he was so taken up with his own pains that he had no time to think of his murdered family."

The Big Captain carried him to his own wig-wam, where he lay two and twenty moons before he could walk with crutches. When he grew able, his business was to light the Big Captain's pipe, and fetch water for him. In this last occupation he sometimes met at the spring, American white women, whose families mostly had been murdered, and who were now slaves of the Shawanese. One of these he knew; she had lived in Ohio, and her story was that of hundreds of others, whose husbands and children had been surprised at their firesides and murdered. Bird promised should he ever live to escape, that he would give information of the fate of these unhappy women, whose number in this single village was fifty-eight, and who, doubtless, had long been considered dead.

The Indians are the most jealous and suspicious of their prisoners of any people in the world. One of them had observed this conversation, without overhearing it, and gave notice that there was a plot among the white slaves to run away. Bird and the poor woman were then brought before the Big Captain, and threatened with death if they did not confess their plots. He persisted in refusing to make any disclosures, and the Big Captain ordered his two thumb nails to be twisted off. Finding that Bird still refused to make any disclosures, he at last became convinced of his innocence, and by way of satisfaction, directed him to twist off the thumb nails of the accuser. This, however, he declined.

From the time that Bird had left off his crutches he had meditated making his escape, although in general he was treated pretty well by the Big Captain, except when the chief was in liquor. At such times even his wife did not dare to come near him, for his passions were terrible, and he was accustomed to endulge them with impunity, because it is a law of the Indians, that a drunken person is not accountable for his actions. It is the liquor, and not the man, that is to blame. In order to throw the Big Captain off his guard Bird affected, on all occasions, to prefer being the slave of such a great warrior to living among the white men, and working hard all day like a beast. "I lied," said Bird; "I don't deny it, but thought it excusable in this case." The Big Captain, however, was very suspicious, and would never give him a chance to escape.

One evening in the latter part of February, when Bird had been nearly forty moons a prisoner, the Big Captain and Lady both got very drunk, and as the rivers were now frozen, he resolved to take advantage of this circumstance to attempt gaining Detroit, or some other settlement of the whites. He had from time to time, by little and little, furnished his knapsack with a good quantity of jerked venison to serve him in his long journey. On the night of one of the last days of February, 1815, he left the Big Captain's wigwam, and took a direction as nearly south as possible, through the woods, in order to strike the shores of lake Erie. There was an Indian path to the lake, but did not dare to take that for fear of being overtaken by the Indians, should they discover his absence. It was a cold moonlight night, yet still he found much difficulty in keeping a direct course, and it was broad daylight before he struck the lake. From thence he continued up the lake, until about twelve o'clock, and had got, as they told him afterwards, about thirty miles from the town, when he was seized by a party of five Indians, as he was sitting on a log eating a piece of jerked venison. The Big Captain had discovered his flight at day light, and set off with three hundred men, divided into parties of five each, to scour the woods in every direction.

They tied his hands behind him, and drove him in this way about a mile, to a rising ground, where they fired their guns, and lighted a fire, by setting fire to an old walnut tree, as signals for the other parties to come in. Here they passed the night, during which about one half of the parties had come in. The morning after they drove Bird into the town, and a council was called to decide on what was to be done with him. It was concluded upon, that as he was determined not to stay with them, he should be " *burnt three days.*" The famous Shawanese Prophet, brother to Tecumseh, was at the council; his opinions are of great weight with the Shawanese, as he was considered to speak the will of the Great Spirit. Bird has seen him often. He was about fifty, very ill looking, and no warrior. He was continually exhorting the Indians to fight the Americans, and keep them away from their lands. The influence of the prophet may be estimated by the fact that at one time he prevailed upon some of the tribes to abstain from spirituous liquors; but they afterwards returned to their old habits.

The Big Captain came to tell Bird what they were going to do with him. It was what he expected, and had made up his mind to it.— About an hour after sunrise he was taken a little outside of the village to the war-dance ground, where he supposes three or four hundred Indians had collected. They tied him down on his back, with his feet fastened to a stake, and the Big Captain seized a firebrand, which he held first against his hand, then against his arm, taunting him, at the same time, by asking "if he intended to run away again soon." This was done by others in turn, for thirteen different times, at intervals of half an hour, so that he might be as susceptible as possible to pain. The intervals were filled up with dancings and expressions of contempt for the white men. The louder he groaned, the louder they shouted, exclaiming that "Indians never groaned, but the white man was no better than a woman." This ceremony continued till within about two hours of sunset, at which time the fingers of his right hand were almost consumed, and his arm burnt quite to the bone. I saw his hand and arm myself, or I could never have been brought to believe that human nature could have endured such long suffering.

At this time there came up one Randall M'Donald, a Scotch trader from Quebec. He had been all through that country buying furs, and was now on his way home, with his caravan of sixteen mules and four horses loaded with skins: He was well known to the Indians, and offered to purchase Bird for a gallon of rum, which he told the Big Captain would afford them a much better frolic than burning a poor white man. The bargain was struck—the Big Captain took the rum—Randall M'Donald, with his own hands cut Bird loose, put him on one of his horses, and set out immediately. They travelled all night, for fear the Indians would repent their bargain after drinking the liquor, and reclaim the poor half burned victim. In nine days Bird thinks they reached Kingston, where Randall bought him some clothes, and got a surgeon to attend him. They staid four days at Kingston, and then went down to Quebec. All the time during this journey he was attended by Randall, who took him home to his house in Quebec, employed a surgeon, and he soon got well enough to travel on foot. The good Scotchman then told him he might take his choice, either to remain with him or go home. Bird chose the latter; and Randall gave him money to carry him to the frontier; and sent him off with his good wishes.

In these miserable times of national antipathies and savage warfare, it is gratifying to trace, in the conduct of Randall M'Donald, that steady, untiring benevolence, which adorns and exalts our nature. That he should have saved the prisoner at the stake is nothing. But that he should carry him with him, and support him through such a long, tedious journey, dress his wounds in the wilderness, afterwards take him to his home, and finally give him money to support him till he got to his own country, is what, I fear, few could have done under like circumstances. Let us, then, do honor to this benevolent Scotchman, who saved one of our citizens from the stake and sent him safe to his home.

The money given him by Randall M'Donald lasted Bird till he came to Vermont; from whence to Washington, he subsisted on the benevolence of his countrymen. In general, he says, he had little to complain of. His story almost always gained him food and lodging, and, with very few exceptions, he was seldom turned away from any man's door.— Misery and poverty so seldom knock at the doors of an American farmer, that his heart is not yet steeled to apathy by becoming familiar with objects of distress. From the borders of Vermont, he traveled by land to Albany, where the Patroon* got him a passage, free, to Egg-Harbour, and he says he thought his lady never would have done sending provisions on board the vessel for him. From Egg-Harbour, he came across New-Jersey to Delaware Bay, which he crossed to Jones's creek in the state of Delaware, whence he went to Haddaway's ferry, crossed the Chesapeake to Annapolis, and arrived at Washington the 6th day of July, 1815. His object in going there was to fulfil his promise to the poor woman of the old Shawanese Town. It is with pleasure I add, that he was admitted to an audience of the President, and that measures have been taken, by the proper authority, to recover these unfortunate captives, should they be still alive.

* *Stephen Van Ranselaer, Esq. of Albany, commonly known by this title in New-York state.*

I saw him, and enquired particularly into his story, which he repeated as I have given it, without variation or embellishment. There was a striking manliness in his deportment, and he told his tale with such an air of simple truth, that I could swear to every word of it. I asked if he had any objection to its being made public? He said none, provided I did not make a fine story about him. He was going among some distant relations in Fredrick county, who he said would take care of him as long as he lived, and he did not want them to think he wished to be the hero of a story. He had more than forty wounds—his shoulder was partly cut off—his thigh gashed with seams—his side scarred with a tomahawk—his fingers almost burnt off—and one of his arms, in some places, nearly bare to the bone. Yet, he neither repined or complained that his lot was harder than that of other men, but exhibited, more than any being I ever saw, an example of that philosophy which is the offspring, not of reasoning, but of suffering, and of that inflexible hardihood which a long succession of labors, dangers and hardships ever inspires.

COLOPHON

The text of this booklet is machine set in 14 point Baskerville. The running heads, folios, etc. are hand set in 18 point Bologna from the Stephenson, Blake foundry in Sheffield, England. Some *125* copies were printed on 65 pound Hammermill Ripple cover stock to be hard bound, and *150* copies were printed on thin Bristol cover on a smaller page size, to be put in paper binding. The colors are terra cotta, bluegreen and aqua.
This is copy number *105* in paper cover.

Glen Adams, printer.
April, 1973.

NARRATIVE

OF

HENRY BIRD,

Who was carried away by the Indians, after the murder of his whole family, in 1811, and held in Captivity:—His sufferings, and rescue from the Savage Monsters, in 1815, while burning at the stake.

PRINTED AT BRIDGEPORT, NOVEMBER 1815.

NARRATIVE
OF
HENRY BIRD,

Who was carried away by the Indians, after the murder of his whole family, in 1811, and held in Captivity:—His sufferings, and rescue from the Savage Monsters, in 1815, while burning at the stake.

PRINTED AT BRIDGEPORT, NOVEMBER 1815.